GW00391745

Alvaro del Portillo

The Power of Humility

by
Helena Scott and Ethel Tolansky

*All booklets are published thanks to the
generous support of the members of the
Catholic Truth Society*

CATHOLIC TRUTH SOCIETY
PUBLISHERS TO THE HOLY SEE

2

Contents

Inside images: © Opus Dei Information Office.

All rights reserved. First published 2014 by The Incorporated Catholic Truth Society, 40-46 Harleyford Road London SE11 5AY Tel: 020 7640 0042 Fax: 020 7640 0046. © 2014 The Incorporated Catholic Truth Society.

ISBN 978 1 86082 902 4

Beginnings

This is the priest I would like to imitate!

One day in the early 1980s a young man was praying in front of the statue of Our Lady in the Cathedral of Notre Dame in Paris. His name was Louis and he was from Cameroon. While he was there a white-haired priest came up to him and introduced himself, and they were soon deep in conversation. Louis was very struck by this fatherly-looking priest, with a gentle smile and understanding eyes, who spoke with such faith, warmth, priestly zeal and love for Jesus Christ. After they had both returned to their respective countries, they kept in touch by letter, and Louis discovered his own vocation to the priesthood. He entered the seminary and was ordained in 1989. Referring to that encounter, Father Louis said later: "This is my model, this is the priest I would like to imitate!" The priest who had inspired him, and continues to do so, along his path in the priesthood, was Alvaro del Portillo.

A family man

It might seem odd to call a Catholic priest and later bishop, a "family man" by nature. Bishop Alvaro del Portillo was, like every good Catholic priest, a "father". He came from a big family himself - he was the third of eight children, born

Bishop Alvaro talks to Opus Dei members and friends.

in Madrid on 11th March 1914 to Clementina and Ramon del Portillo. Clementina, originally from Mexico, was a full-time wife and mother; Ramon was a lawyer working for an insurance company. Both were devout, practising Catholics, and they did their best to give all their children a thorough grounding in Christianity as lived out in daily life. Alvaro was always great friends with his father, an earnest, cultivated man who was serious without being severe. The family prayed the Rosary together every day, and the children were not compelled to join in, but did so anyway, because they wanted to. After Alvaro made his First Holy Communion at the age of seven, he followed his mother's example and started going to Mass every day, before setting off for school, and not just on Sundays.

The importance of the love and support of a family was something that stayed with him all his life. In his case, as the successor of St Josemaria Escriva at the head of Opus Dei, his children were, first and foremost, the faithful of Opus Dei, and second, anyone who needed his help. But Alvaro del Portillo not only loved and looked after all his spiritual sons and daughters like the best of fathers; he needed them. He needed to have them with him, needed to live as part of a family with all the give-and-take that this involves. He saw himself as being constantly helped and supported by his children. He relied on their prayers, not just as a pious cliché, but in the actual day-to-day reality of his life. He needed their affection, help, co-operation and feedback in his work of governing Opus Dei and stimulating the spread of its apostolate around the world.

Choosing a career

When it was time for Alvaro to think about his career, he chose engineering, which required several years of hard study and demanding technical training, starting at the age of fifteen. In 1933, aged nineteen, he passed the entrance exam into engineering school, one of only 23 to succeed out of 549 applicants. Friends from school remembered him as a cheerful, friendly and very kind boy; and even as an adolescent he displayed the simplicity and genuine humility that came to characterise him in later life. As well as sports, he enjoyed reading and photography. He had a gift for languages and for drawing. He continued to practise his faith, and found his relationship with God helped and strengthened by seeing the beauty of nature, particularly during family holidays. He realised later on that God was already at work in his soul during this time.

One summer, during a family holiday on the north coast of Spain, Alvaro, one of his brothers, and some friends decided to take a trip by motorboat over the bay to a nearby town. As they were on the boat waiting to start, his brother started feeling ill, and Alvaro gave up the sea-trip, taking his brother back to look after him. Later that day they heard to their horror that the boat had been caught unexpectedly in a violent storm and had capsized, and all the people on board except one had been drowned. As he prayed for his friends' souls, it occurred to Alvaro that God might have left him in this world for a reason: there might be something definite that God had in mind for him.

After engineering school Alvaro went on to start his university degree in engineering; but things did not go as planned. This was the early 1930s, and the worldwide recession was hitting hard. The Del Portillo family, like so many others, was in considerable difficulties. To help his parents cope, Alvaro opted to take a degree in public works, which was a shorter course than engineering, so that he could gain paid employment, though at a fairly low level, as soon as possible. To begin with, he studied both courses simultaneously, and academically he managed very well. However, the college authorities soon told him that he had to opt for one course or the other. He dropped the engineering degree, aiming to resume it later on.

During term-time he started attending a conference of the St Vincent de Paul society, an international Christian voluntary organisation dedicated to tackling poverty and disadvantage by providing direct practical assistance to anyone in need. They met once a week for spiritual reading, followed by a discussion of the results of the previous week's visits, the needs they had encountered, and plans for the coming week. The inspiration behind this was the wish to put their faith into practice in deeds of social solidarity to help alleviate the dire poverty in which so many people were forced to live. Alvaro did not take his own circumstances (relatively easy, compared with the families living in slums) for granted, but wanted to make use of what he had in order to help others. He made a deep and lasting impression on other members of the group, who saw how intelligent and kind he was, and how much he loved God and other people.

In those viciously anti-clerical times, it took a lot of courage for a group of young Christian men to go into the Madrid slums to teach catechism classes and offer help in the name of their faith. In February 1934, Alvaro and four or five others had gone to teach their regular catechism class in the Vallecas district of Madrid. When they left the class to go home, a group of men jumped on them to beat them up, quite clearly intending to kill them. Alvaro was hit on the head with a heavy spanner. He only escaped because the attack took place close to an underground station, and he and his companions, covered in blood, were able to dodge into the station and onto a train just as the doors were closing. When he got home, unwilling to alarm his family, Alvaro told them calmly that he had simply tripped over in the street, but the head wound caused him a lot of trouble and pain before it finally healed.

Meeting St Josemaria

In March 1935 one of the members of the St Vincent de Paul group introduced Alvaro, then just twenty-one, to Father Josemaria Escriva. Father Escriva, who had founded Opus Dei (Latin for "work of God", often simply called "the Work" by its members) seven years earlier, was at that point carrying out pastoral work in Madrid, running a small hall of residence for students in Ferraz Street, and ministering to the poor and sick. Alvaro thought he was a very joyful-looking young priest, and wanted to know more of him, but though they arranged to meet a second time, they missed each other. Four months later, just before going away on holiday, Alvaro decided to go and visit Father Escriva in Ferraz Street again, and was promptly invited to a day of recollection - not something he had ever done before - the following day. It was a turning-point in his life. "That morning, 7th July 1935," he recalled later, "the Holy Spirit opened my eyes. He used a spiritual retreat preached by our Founder to awaken a new restlessness in my heart, which led me to begin my *real* life." He asked to join Opus Dei that very day, and from then on committed himself heart and soul to his new calling.

Alvaro learned later that, although his vocation had come to him as a sudden revelation, Father Escriva had been praying for him by name for several years before they actually met. Escriva knew one of Alvaro's aunts, and she had spoken about her nephew in glowing terms. Alvaro was not the sort of person who takes hasty decisions without thinking them over thoroughly beforehand. In this case, God had been leading and preparing him, and he had responded faithfully to the graces he had been given, especially through the sacraments, to the point where he was able to recognise and embrace the call to commit his life to God in Opus Dei as soon as he heard it clearly.

Alvaro now needed to discover exactly what the spirit of Opus Dei consisted of and how to make it part of his daily life in his own circumstances. Instead of going away as he had planned, he remained in Madrid until 22nd August in order to receive regular classes from St Josemaria in the Ferraz Street residence, about the spirit and practice of Opus Dei. In these he was soon joined by another newcomer to Opus Dei, Jose Maria Hernandez Garnica.

First steps in Opus Dei

Father Josemaria had no need to give the two young men basic Christian instruction, as they had both received thorough religious education in their families and at school. Instead, he explained to them how to sanctify their work and study by doing it well and conscientiously, so that it was intense, constant, properly organised, and well finished off; by doing it to please God and not for their own self-satisfaction; and by offering it to God for specific intentions - for their families and friends, for the other faithful in Opus Dei and the founder himself, for the Pope and the Church, for the local bishop and his intentions, for the Holy Souls, for someone with a particular need, etc.

Father Josemaria explained the practice of the presence of God; how to do meditation and mental prayer every day; and how to punctuate the day with regular devotions or acts of piety, such as the Rosary, the Angelus, paying a visit to the Blessed Sacrament, spiritual reading, and above all Holy Mass, putting love into all of them. In the classes he also explained how they should make a brief but effective daily examination of conscience, and showed them the meaning and practice of mortification and penance in ordinary life:

"That joke, that witty remark held on the tip of your tongue; the cheerful smile for those who annoy you; that silence when you're unjustly accused; your friendly conversation with people whom you find boring and tactless; the daily effort to overlook one irritating detail or another in the people who live with you... this, with perseverance, is indeed solid interior mortification... Choose mortifications that don't mortify others... Conquer yourself each day from the very first moment, getting up on the dot, at a fixed time, without yielding a single minute to laziness."

Christian apostolate

In particular, Father Escriva explained to Alvaro and Jose Maria about Christian apostolate, why it was part and parcel of the Christian vocation, and how to carry out apostolate with their own friends, family and classmates. Apostolate, as Father Escriva helped them to see, was an "overflowing of the interior life", the natural result of a close, faithful, personal relationship with Jesus Christ. It was based on friendship and mutual respect, trust and confidence, and consisted of sharing with others, normally on a one-to-one basis, the happiness of getting to know Christ and following him more closely.

All of these ideas, and many more, were based on a steadily growing familiarity with the life of Christ himself, nourished by regular, meditative reading of the Gospel. St Josemaria Escriva showed them how they could fall in love with Jesus Christ, who is Love, and model their lives on his, right where they were, living in the middle of the world, sharing in Christ's hunger to redeem souls. Alvaro knew very well that God was not calling him to join a religious order, much though he respected and venerated the holy religious whom he knew or heard about. The vocation to Opus Dei that he had seen and embraced was God's call to follow him in the middle of the world, as the first twelve Apostles had done, by sanctifying his ordinary daily life and carrying out apostolate. Faith, hope, charity, humility, poverty, and the other virtues he was aiming to develop, were based on and expressed through what Father Escriva called the "human virtues", which included order and tidiness, diligence, cheerfulness, responsibility, honesty, loyalty and generosity.

Father Escriva was a gifted communicator, and his words fell on fertile soil. Alvaro was filled with enthusiasm as he found that what he was hearing in the classes fulfilled a deep need and gave every aspect of his life a whole new meaning. In response, he methodically set about applying the advice to his daily life, learning how to find God in his studies and in the people around him, and how to listen for and respond to the touches of the Holy Spirit in his soul. He was grateful to the very end of his life for having first learned the spirit and practice of Opus Dei directly from its founder.

Towards the end of August Alvaro left Madrid to join his family on holiday, keeping in regular contact with Father Escriva by letter. He continued his efforts to stay close to God throughout the day, and made the most of the opportunities offered on holiday for encouraging his friends to practise their faith more deeply.

Enthusiasm

After a time, as always happens, Alvaro found that his initial enthusiasm, and the effortless awareness of God's presence in everything, had disappeared. It was not that he was going through a spiritual crisis; simply that the spontaneous zest which had made his first steps seem easy, was no longer there. He told Father Escriva about this disconcerting change, and was soon reassured. Father Escriva helped him to see that he needed to act not out of enthusiasm but out of love, shouldering his obligations, and that this necessarily involved self-denial. This made perfect sense to Alvaro, and he took it to heart, applying himself day after day to the effort of conversing with God in prayer, sanctifying his work, making the best use of his time, and developing his spirit of service, charity and patience towards others.

One day his youngest brother, Carlos, got into Alvaro's room when he was out and started playing with some of his papers - which were in fact engineering designs on which he had spent a good part of the past year - tearing and spoiling them. Their mother found what Carlos had done and warned him, "When Alvaro gets home, he'll be furious!" But when Alvaro came in and saw what had happened, he did not lose his temper. Instead, he sat Carlos on his knee and explained to him how long he had spent on producing the designs, and how Carlos, by playing where he shouldn't have, had caused all that time to be wasted. Carlos, young as he was, never forgot his brother's remarkably patient reaction in place of the angry telling-off he had expected.

Because of Alvaro's determined, methodical efforts to absorb and practise all he was learning from Father Josemaria, he developed very quickly into someone who could be relied upon to pass on the spirit of Opus Dei to others. In April 1936 Father Josemaria went to Valencia for several weeks to see about opening another students' residence there, leaving Alvaro in Madrid to take over the task of giving Christian formation to the students in the Ferraz Street residence.

During the War

Spanish Civil War

Soon after this, in July 1936, the Spanish Civil War broke out and lasted until April 1939. As Catholics in the anti-religious "Republican" zone of Spain, Alvaro, his family, and the other faithful of Opus Dei were in constant danger of arrest and summary execution. The story has been told in detail elsewhere, and here it is enough to say that Alvaro not only maintained his faith but developed his relationship with our Lord, and his understanding of and love for his vocation to Opus Dei, still more under these outwardly harsh and often terrifying circumstances, and gave considerable moral support to St Josemaria at different points in their adventures. "Providentially, and constantly, there have never been lacking brothers of yours who were like a father rather than sons to me, when I stood in need of a father's consolation and strength," St Josemaria wrote later, understood by all to refer primarily to Alvaro.

His father, Ramon del Portillo, was arrested; his mother, being a Mexican citizen, took refuge in the Mexican Embassy for a few days; Alvaro, to avoid being forced to join the "Republican" army, hid in the Finnish Embassy, but was soon arrested himself. He was held in prison for two months until the end of January

1937, remaining calm and cheerful even though he was subjected to hunger and atrocious ill-treatment and there was every possibility of summary execution. He prayed hard and concentrated on forgiving his tormentors from his heart, and helping his fellow-prisoners. When he was released, with no explanation, he re-joined his mother who was living on premises belonging to the Mexican Embassy. At the beginning of March he moved into the Honduran Legation where St Josemaria and others were also living, in cramped conditions and with very little to eat. His father was released from prison, probably because he was so ill he was not expected to live, and although Alvaro's mother cared for her husband as best she could, he grew steadily worse and died on 14th October that year. To Alvaro's great sorrow, he was not able to leave the Honduran Legation to see his father or comfort his mother, because of the near-certainty that he would be re-arrested and put back in prison or executed. His mother left Madrid with her younger children and eventually reached Marseilles in France. Alvaro left the Honduran Consulate at the beginning of July 1938 and, with two companions, enlisted in the Republican Army with false papers. They reached the battlefront after several months, and were able to cross over to the other side, in a way that was clearly providential if not downright miraculous, on 12th October. They made their way to Burgos to join St Josemaria, who had escaped earlier by a different route.

Apostolate of friendship

Throughout his life, Alvaro made friends easily. People were attracted by his unselfish behaviour and his kindness, which led him to take endless trouble to help others, and by his calm but determined approach to problems and difficulties. As they got to know him better, they came to realise that these characteristics were based on a very deep interior life, nourished by prayer and the Sacraments, and constant recourse to God as his loving Father. In October 1938, after joining St Josemaria in the "National" zone of Spain and being conscripted into the army, Alvaro was sent on a short military training course near Burgos. He managed to find a church where he could attend Mass every day, setting off very early in the morning and returning in time for the morning inspection. His comrades on the training course were both impressed and interested, and by the time the course ended a few weeks later, about thirty of them were going to Mass with him every day.

Studying languages

At the same time, at St Josemaria's suggestion, and using whatever time he could find, he took up the study of Japanese, English, French and German in order to be ready to travel to one or more foreign countries after the conflict was over to plant the seed of Opus Dei's apostolates there. He had a natural gift for languages, and he applied to this work, and to other areas of study as time went on, the habits he had acquired as a student of engineering: he was methodical, orderly, rigorous and precise in the way he studied.

Hard work

However, the Second World War started less than five months after the end of the Spanish Civil War in 1939, and although Spain was not directly involved, it was not possible to travel to any of the proposed countries. Back in Madrid, Alvaro worked as a civil engineer, helped St Josemaria with the task of running the students' residence and teaching Christian formation to students, travelled on overnight trains to other cities at weekends to teach more people - especially students - about loving God in and through their ordinary working lives, and studied for a doctorate in history. He completed his doctoral thesis on the early exploration of the Californian coast in 1944; it was a huge amount of work. Alvaro had a remarkable capacity for work, and he developed this capacity, as well as his powers of memory and concentration, throughout his life, simply for love of God. He once said:

> "If we want to find more time to work, we need a greater consciousness of God's presence. Then we will work more peacefully and more intensely, and with a greater desire to do things well. The result is that our time multiplies, because we do things better, with more

zest, and are keener to get them right. Therefore we
have fewer distractions and we waste less time."

Calling to the priesthood

For some time St Josemaria had been conscious of the need
for priests who were imbued with the spirit of Opus Dei, so
that they could preach and give spiritual direction to people
of Opus Dei and those who were attracted to its apostolate,
and help them to put its spirit into practice. He could not
see how this could come about, but was convinced that
God would show him when the time was ripe. In 1940,
meanwhile, he asked Alvaro, Jose Maria Hernandez
Garnica, and a third Opus Dei man, Jose Luis Muzquiz, to
begin studying for the priesthood. Each of them, freely, said
yes, they were ready to become priests; they recognised
God's will for them in St Josemaria's request.

Alvaro was then 25 years old, and to all appearances
had a distinguished career ahead of him as a civil engineer.
Without hesitation, he laid it aside in order to follow this
new manifestation of God's will for his life.

In agreement with the Bishop of Madrid, the three
candidates for the priesthood did not enter the diocesan
seminary, although they studied the same philosophy and
theology subjects, and took the same exams as the other
seminarians. St Josemaria arranged for them to be taught
by some of the teachers from ecclesiastical universities in

Rome who had come to Madrid to escape the ravages of the Second World War. They combined these classes, studying and exams with all the other work they were doing, and still managed to gain high marks in the seminary exams.

In February 1943 St Josemaria received the answer to his prayers, with the realisation that men of Opus Dei could be ordained as members of a new priestly association which he would set up as a "society of common life without vows", in the canonical terminology then in force. He gave it the name of "The Priestly Society of the Holy Cross". Having obtained the full approval of the Bishop of Madrid, he asked Alvaro to travel to Rome to present the necessary documentation in person to the Holy See. It was May 1943, and Rome had not yet been overrun by the Nazis. Alvaro had an eventful but successful journey in a small aircraft, arriving in Rome on 25th May. He had a private audience with Pope Pius XII on 4th June. For this important day Alvaro wore the full dress uniform of the Spanish Engineers Corps, complete with gold buttons and a purple sash. He was just twenty-nine at the time. As the story goes, when Alvaro entered the Vatican through the Bronze Doors, the officer in charge, taking Alvaro for a high-ranking visiting military official, lined the Swiss Guards up for review. Alvaro, not missing a beat, returned the officer's salute, reviewed the guards and strode upstairs to the audience hall.

Rome and the 'Rock'

Audience with the Pope

Fully aware of his responsibilities, Alvaro spoke to Pope Pius XII with deep reverence, but also with clarity and conviction, about the message of Opus Dei: achieving genuine personal holiness in the middle of the world. He explained in great detail who the people of Opus Dei were, and the reasons for their application to set up a new society for priests, as the Holy Father listened encouragingly and prompted him with searching questions. The audience went well, and the Holy Father was much impressed by him. The result was the papal approval of the Priestly Society of the Holy Cross. Alvaro also met and made friends with several other church dignitaries during the time he spent in Rome. He returned to Madrid on 21st June, and on 11th October the Holy See gave permission for the establishment of the Priestly Society of the Holy Cross at diocesan level.

Ordination to the priesthood

Alvaro was ordained to the priesthood, together with Jose Maria and Jose Luis, by the Bishop of Madrid on 25th June 1944. Taught by St Josemaria, he saw the priesthood as a participation in the one priesthood of Christ, a very special identification with Christ, and a role of unconditional service towards everyone - just as Christ "did not come to be served, but to serve". From then on, the greatest joy and privilege of his life was to celebrate Mass daily, which he did with heartfelt devotion, and to administer the other Sacraments, especially the Sacrament of Reconciliation.

Later he wrote:

"What do people want, what do they expect of the priest, the minister of Christ, the living sign of the presence of the Good Shepherd? We would venture to say that, although they may not explicitly say so, they need, want and hope for a priest-priest, a priest through and through, a man who gives his life for them, by opening to them the horizons of the soul; a man who unceasingly exercises his ministry, whose heart is capable of understanding and loving everyone even though he may at times be rejected; a man who gives simply and joyfully, in season and even out of season (cf. 2 *Tm* 4:2), what he alone can give: the richness of grace, of divine intimacy which, through him, God wishes to distribute among men."

Saxum, a rock

As early as 1939, when the Spanish Civil War had just ended, and Alvaro was twenty-five, Father Josemaria had written to him in a letter dated 23rd March: "May Jesus watch over you, *Saxum* [Latin for rock]. And yes, that is

With Saint Josemaria in Opus Dei's central house in Rome.

what you are. I see that the Lord is giving you strength and making this word of mine, 'Saxum', operative in you. Thank him for this and remain faithful to him…"

What does it mean to be called a "rock"? It implies strength, dependability, support; when someone leans on a rock, it does not collapse. How and why did Alvaro acquire this nickname so early on in Opus Dei, having joined just four years earlier? In those four years, three of which were taken up by the Spanish Civil War, Father Josemaria had seen and experienced Alvaro's loyalty, his unswerving faithfulness to God's will and his complete disregard of self in carrying it out. He was always positive when the future looked bleak, always unflappable during the crises of the war, and in the difficult post-war times. Father Josemaria had found him to be a young man of deep, practical faith, who was reliable, cheerful, and despite his youth, a man who could help him in the development and progress of the Work then and in the future.

For the whole of his life, Alvaro gave total support, loyalty and faithfulness to St Josemaria. His capacity for generous obedience was not the sign of a weak character. He embodied to the full the paradox that St Josemaria pointed to in his book *The Way*: "Temper your will, strengthen your will: with God's grace, let it be like a sword of steel. Only by being strong-willed can you know how not to be so in order to obey." St Josemaria could not work with sycophants or yes-men: he needed the support offered in freedom by people who each had a strong personality of their own, and above all, a solid life of prayer.

The growth of Opus Dei within Spain soon made it necessary for St Josemaria to apply for canonical recognition of his new foundation from the Holy See. This was especially important, first because people of Opus Dei were going to start its apostolate in other countries (some went to Portugal and Italy in 1946 to open Opus Dei centres there); and second, because its growth had given rise to suspicion and attacks from people who did not understand this new message, saw it as heretical, or thought it somehow aimed at undermining the religious orders. Father Alvaro, together with the other faithful in Opus Dei, gave all the support he could to St Josemaria Escriva in these trying circumstances - as did the Bishop of Madrid, the spiritual director of the Madrid seminary, and the Abbot of the shrine of Montserrat in Barcelona, among others. Now, early in 1946, Father Alvaro was asked by Father Escriva to travel to Rome again, this time to request official recognition for Opus Dei at pontifical level from the Holy See. In view of the total novelty of Opus Dei's message about holiness in the middle of the world, this was not a simple matter.

Official recognition by the Holy See

In Rome, as always, Father Alvaro worked hard, meeting cardinals from different countries who had come to

Rome for a consistory, telling them all about Opus Dei, and obtaining letters of recommendation in support of the application to the Holy See. However, after over three months, it was clear to him that Father Escriva, as the founder, would have to come to Rome himself if any progress was to be made. This he did in June, and their combined work was successful to a relative extent. Opus Dei was recognised by the Holy See as a Secular Institute in February 1947, and although this definition did not fully match the nature of Opus Dei, it was sufficient for the time being to enable them to continue with spreading in new countries the call to holiness through ordinary work. The first people of Opus Dei had already come to the UK at the end of 1946, and were living in London.

Moving to Rome

Meanwhile Cardinal Montini, the future Pope Paul VI, had suggested to St Josemaria Escriva that he ought to move to Rome and make Opus Dei's headquarters there. They had virtually no money, but St Josemaria and Father Alvaro, placing their trust firmly in God, asked family members, friends and acquaintances for help and explored every avenue of possible funding. They succeeded in acquiring, providentially, a property in the Parioli district of Rome. They put down a deposit on the house, consisting of some gold coins which had been a gift to St Josemaria, and which he had been hoping to have melted down and made into a chalice; the agreement stipulated that the coins should be returned once the property had been paid for. As Andres Vazquez de Prada stated in his book *The Founder of Opus Dei*, Volume III, referring to the acquisition of the property: "Who else but Don Alvaro would have tried to buy a mansion with nothing but a few gold coins and total faith in the founder?" And who but he could have succeeded?

Then came the huge task of renovating, restructuring and building afresh, to provide a place that would serve as Opus Dei's headquarters and a centre for its apostolate. They named the new centre "Villa Tevere", Tevere being the Italian for Tiber, the name of the river that runs through Rome. They themselves lived in the most absolute poverty, for which the harsh war years in Spain had been some preparation. Father Josemaria and Father Alvaro, and the other Opus Dei people living with them, worked, studied, and endured the hunger, extremes of heat and cold, and other discomforts of those early years in Rome, seeing God's hand in the difficulties and knowing that their sacrifices were, through God's kindness, winning many graces for souls.

Paying the builders

Father Alvaro was personally in charge of fund-raising to pay the builders who were working on the new premises. Once again, his faith in God's providence, and his own unsparing work, enabled him to ensure that the builders were paid punctually at the end of each week's work. This matter was a huge burden for him, but instead of seeing the builders as antagonists, he made friends with them, got to know their personal and family circumstances, and was perfectly aware that they needed their weekly pay to put food on the table at home. Whenever one of them put in an extra effort, beyond what they were contracted to do, Father Alvaro would add a generous tip to his weekly pay packet.

In 1948, on top of all this work, he became rector of the newly-established Roman College of the Holy Cross, where Opus Dei men from around the world studied a three-year theology course, many of them going on to be ordained to the priesthood. The college started out in Villa Tevere itself, functioning there for many years until it was moved to larger premises just outside Rome. Father Alvaro also found, or rather made, time to study for a degree in Canon Law, and later successfully presented his thesis for a doctorate.

Social project at Salto di Fondi

As rector, Father Alvaro realised that one of the most urgent needs for his students was a place where they could go to get away from the heat of Rome in the long summer months. A friend of his had a property which he wanted to sell, part of which seemed to be just what was needed. It was called Salto di Fondi and was on the coast, halfway between Rome and Naples. It was a huge agricultural estate, worked by around 300 farm labourers. Thinking about these people and their families, Father Alvaro came up with an unusual project. He obtained loans to buy the property, divided it up into smaller areas, and then made arrangements with the bank for the labourers to be able to buy the land they worked on for affordable prices, by paying small sums over a period of several years. In that way the former hired labourers now owned their land. Father Alvaro retained for Opus Dei one part of the property, which was soon able to supply the Opus Dei members in the city with fresh produce, and which provided a place for the students to go and rest during the heat of the summer.

A Quiet Servant of the Church

Serving the Church

During the pontificate of Pius XII, Father Alvaro was appointed to different posts in the Roman Curia. One post came after another. In 1949 he was appointed a member of the commission of the committee planning the Holy Year of 1950. Also under Pius XII he was appointed consultor of the Sacred Congregation of Religious, and as time went on his reputation for dedicated, faithful hard work and intelligence increased, and he came to be highly regarded in the Roman Curia for his personal qualities, his pastoral experience, his solid theological background and his legal expertise.

Pope Pius XII died on 9th October 1958, and at the end of that month Mgr Roncalli, the Patriarch of Venice, was elected Pope, taking the name of John XXIII. The following year he announced that there would be a second Vatican Council. He already knew Father Alvaro del Portillo and Opus Dei well, and would call upon him to work for the Council in the service of the Church. Pope John XXIII did not live to the end of the Second Vatican Council, but it was continued by his successor, Pope Paul VI.

Working for the Second Vatican Council

In May 1959 Father Alvaro was appointed Consultor of the Congregation of the Council. In August, he was appointed President of the Commission on the Laity in the pre-preparatory phase of the Council. Next, he was appointed a member of the pre-preparatory Commission on the States of Perfection, and a member of the third Commission of the Congregation of the Council, charged with studying the new means of apostolate in the modern world. In October 1962 he was appointed a "peritus" or expert to be officially consulted by the Vatican Council, and in November he was specifically appointed a peritus of the Commission for the Discipline of the Clergy and Christian People. Almost immediately afterwards he was appointed secretary of this same commission. Between 29th September and December 1963, during the second session of the Vatican Council, this commission was asked to synthesise all the work it had done into a single document, which was approved by the Council as the decree *Presbyterorum Ordinis*, the Decree on the Ministry and Life of Priests.

Together with all this, Father Alvaro was appointed consultor of the Commission for Bishops and the Goverment of Dioceses, and of the Commission for the Religious. Afterwards, he was qualifier for the Supreme Congregation of the Holy Office and consultor for the

Pontifical Commission for the Revision of the Code of Canon Law. He was also a judge of the tribunal for the causes of competence for the Congregation of the Doctrine of the Faith; consultor for the same congregation; secretary of the Commission for Secular Institutes of the Congregation for Religious; and consultor for the Congregation of the Clergy, the Pontifical Commission for Social Communications, and the Congregation for the Causes of the Saints.

"The esteem in which Don Alvaro was held in the Church at large, and in the Roman Curia in particular, grew by the day," stated one of his biographers. The numerous meetings before and during Vatican II meant that Father Alvaro got to know many cardinals, bishops and priests, who were impressed by his openness, helpfulness and fraternity. There was a great deal of work to do, and one of the most difficult and important tasks was to create a friendly, collaborative spirit among ecclesiastics of different ranks, nationalities and outlooks. How did Father Alvaro work with his fellow clergy in order to steer through important decrees? The comments of Cardinal Ciriaci, president of the commission of which Father Alvaro had been the secretary, help to explain how he did it, with reference to the long and difficult discussions on the eventual Vatican II document about the priesthood. "I am well aware of the extent to which this is a result of your prudent, tenacious and courteous efforts. Without failing to respect the freedom of others to have and express their own opinions, you never swerved from the track of fidelity to the great principles of priestly spirituality."

Pope John XXIII had said that the first aim of Vatican II should be to "safeguard and teach the sacred deposit of doctrine in the most effective way", and this was Father Alvaro's guiding principle in all the work he was given to do. Years later, one of those who had worked with him said that in that complex setting, Alvaro del Portillo never took sides, either with "conservatives" or "progressives", but was always simply a man of faith and a man of the Church, and was admired by everyone who knew him. One of the Council Fathers, Cardinal Angelo Dell'Acqua, who had a very sincere regard for him, said that he "wished there could have been many Don Alvaros".

Writings

Two books from Vatican II

Father Alvaro's life grew steadily busier: helping the founder of Opus Dei, travelling with him to encourage the people of Opus Dei in their vocation, working more and more in the Vatican, and coping with recurrent bouts of illness. However, he still found time to study and write.

In his writings, Father Alvaro showed great concern for two particular areas: one, the role of the laity in the Church, and the other the formation and mission of priests. He had gained valuable insights into these areas while working in the Vatican and especially from his work during the Second Vatican Council, and he had prayed and reflected deeply on them. Four years after Vatican II ended, Father Alvaro published *Faithful and Laity in the Church* (1969). He used his knowledge of Canon Law and theology, and his deep supernatural faith, to shed light on Vatican II's teachings about the laity: their role in the Church as the people of God; their important mission in the Church; and the role of the priest who encourages their participation within their particular rights as laity. He discussed these rights as expounded in Canon Law, and highlighted the fact of women having the same rights as men.

With Blessed John Paul II in the Vatican.

In 1970 this book was followed by *On Priesthood: Consecration and Mission of the Priest* - a topic of crucial importance then as now. In this very short book Father Alvaro used not only his deep knowledge of theology, but also his great pastoral experience as a priest, and drew out the practical aspects of Canon Law. According to this book, the key was to understand the depths of meaning of the consecration of the priest and his mission in the Church, and the beauty and importance of priestly holiness.

Introductions to St Josemaria's works

Not usually included in the standard lists of Alvaro del Portillo's publications are the prefaces or forewords that he wrote for the books of spirituality written by St Josemaria. One was for *Christ is Passing By* in 1973, while St Josemaria was still alive; the others were for the posthumously published *Friends of God* (1977), *The Way of the Cross* (1980), *Furrow* (June 1986) and *The Forge* (December 1986). Some of the prefaces are quite long, explaining aspects of St Josemaria's spirituality and how his writings could help the ordinary individual. They all reveal Father Alvaro's own supernatural faith and love for his vocation. When he was ordained a bishop in January 1991, he chose as the motto for his episcopal ministry "*Regnare Christum volumus*" - "We want Christ to reign" - an aspiration often used by St Josemaria. Alvaro del Portillo's books, prefaces and other publications were written for this purpose: service to the Church and apostolate.

With St Josemaria in Guatemala on 19th February 1975, Father Alvaro's name day.

Prelate of Opus Dei

Successor to Father Josemaria Escriva

The Founder of Opus Dei died suddenly on 26th June 1975. It was a huge blow to Father Alvaro, who loved him wholeheartedly as a father. Now a new chapter began in his life. As the General Secretary of Opus Dei, he dealt with the preparations for the funeral, Masses for the repose of the soul (the first of which he celebrated himself) and keeping Opus Dei members all around the world informed of what was being done. He did all this with his customary calm, in spite of his great personal sorrow and sense of loss.

In September that year, at the age of sixty-one, he was elected St Josemaria's successor at the head of Opus Dei. He became the spiritual father of a worldwide family that was growing fast, shouldering the responsibility humbly, but with unhesitating fortitude. From that time onwards he would stress that the foundational times of Mgr Escriva were over and that this new period was one of continuity and fidelity. He himself wanted to go unnoticed and constantly asked for prayers, as St Josemaria had done, in order to carry out his task well. He told Opus Dei members, "Ask God to make me think only as our Father [St Josemaria] thought, and to make me want only what our Father wanted. Then we'll do well." One of his biographers remarked, "He brought souls to God, to the Church, to the founder, and to Opus Dei, but he himself disappeared."

Paul VI and St Josemaria's legacy

In the first audience that Mgr Alvaro del Portillo had with Pope Paul VI, some months after he had become head of Opus Dei, the Holy Father stressed that he should write down details of the life of Mgr Josemaria Escriva. "Everything that has to do with the founder and his doctrinal teachings, both written and oral," the Pope said, "or with the events of his life, no longer belongs solely to Opus Dei. It now forms part of the history of the Church." This was a task that Mgr del Portillo worked at in fidelity to St Josemaria's spirit and with great devotion. He also annotated St Josemaria's personal notebooks, and in January 1986 the annotated copies, together with everything else St Josemaria had written, were given to the Congregation for the Causes of the Saints to study for the process of his beatification.

New projects and fidelity

Mgr del Portillo's humility did not stop him from taking the initiative in starting up the apostolate of Opus Dei in new countries, suggesting new projects and inspiring new developments with a remarkable combination of creativity and loyalty. He said once, "Fidelity is fruitfulness, and therefore it involves imagination, a capacity to invent new ways of doing things, that down-to-earth wisdom which allows us to speak always the same language of God, clothing it in different garments."

Mgr del Portillo kept on with his various tasks in the Vatican and threw himself into continuing Mgr Escriva's work and fulfilling the projects he had had in hand before his death. These included settling the canonical form of Opus Dei, and spreading its apostolate to other countries around the world, in order to offer the beauty and joy of the Catholic faith to those who had not yet received it, and to strengthen the faith and practice of those who had. Mgr del Portillo set about these tasks in the awareness that he was a son of God and so had supernatural grounds for constant hope despite all the difficulties; his inner life was nourished by constant prayer and conversation with God, and trusting love for Our Lady as his mother.

Another goal he set himself was to apply for the cause of beatification and eventual canonisation of Mgr Josemaria Escriva to be opened, and to present his own testimony about the way Escriva had lived.

In 1978, three years after he had become its head, Opus Dei celebrated the fiftieth anniversary of its founding. At the beginning of the year, Mgr del Portillo decided that everyone in Opus Dei would celebrate it as a Marian year, especially dedicated to Our Lady. His confident prayer to our Lady took on a special intensity in the summer, with the death of Pope Paul VI, the election of Pope John Paul I, his sudden and unexpected death a month later, and the election of Pope John Paul II. Mgr del Portillo, who loved and venerated Pope Paul VI, committed each Pope and his intentions and needs to Our Lady's care.

Expansion

"In whatever field of activity, Alvaro del Portillo gave himself to the full, well aware that he participated in the salvific mission of the Church by the faithful fulfilment of his daily duties," declared the Church's "Decree on the heroic virtues of the Servant of God Bishop Alvaro del Portillo". Mgr del Portillo was being asked by bishops from many different countries to send people of Opus Dei there to work and undertake apostolate. He set a demanding pace for the opening of new Opus Dei centres around the world, and in the whole of his time at the head of Opus Dei the average was one new country per year. There was a lot of work to be done once requests had been received from bishops, papal nuncios or the Holy See. Preparatory journeys were made to the countries beforehand to look at possible accommodation and job opportunities for the people who would move there. In Latin America, people of Opus Dei moved to Bolivia in 1978, Honduras in 1980, and Nicaragua in 1992; in the Caribbean, to Trinidad and Tobago in 1983 and the

Dominican Republic in 1988. One of his great dreams was for Opus Dei to reach more countries in Asia and Africa. In French-speaking Africa, Opus Dei centres were opened in DR Congo and Ivory Coast in 1980, and Cameroon in 1988. Opus Dei's apostolate in Asia spread to Hong Kong in 1981, Singapore in 1982, Taiwan in 1985 and Macao in 1989. Another new venture in 1989 was the starting up in New Zealand.

The second half of the 1980s saw the turn of Scandinavia, following a particular suggestion by Pope John Paul II: centres opened in Sweden in 1984 and Finland in 1987. The end of the 1980s brought freedom from Communist rule in Central and Eastern European countries. 1990 saw Opus Dei established in Poland, 1991 the Czech Republic, and 1992 Hungary. On 1st February 1992, returning from a visit to Prague and Budapest, Mgr del Portillo wrote: "We're contributing to the re-Christianising of these places and at the same time we're learning a lot from all these sons and daughters of the Church who have gone through decades of martyrdom." Another of his dreams that came true was the starting up of Opus Dei's apostolate in India in 1993. Here a number of obstacles had to be overcome, one of them being how to obtain residence permits for non-Indian priests. A special joy for him that same year was seeing Opus Dei's work start in Jerusalem.

Pastoral visits: shepherd and father,
in love with Jesus Christ and the Church

During his 19 years of service to the Church as head of
Opus Dei, Mgr del Portillo undertook a large number of
pastoral visits to countries all over the world where people
of Opus Dei were living, and countries where it was
hoped to begin an apostolate in the future. He made these
journeys, sometimes several in the same year, to encourage
the faithful of Opus Dei and strengthen them in their faith,
open up new horizons for their work and apostolate, and
so contribute to the re-Christianisation or evangelisation
of the world. In 1986, responding to Pope John Paul II's
call for the re-evangelisation of Europe, Mgr del Portillo
made a series of short visits to many different European
countries, one after the other.

In 1987 he visited Singapore, Australia, the Philippines,
Hong Kong, Macao, Taiwan, South Korea and Japan. He
also went to mainland China and was able to celebrate
Holy Mass in Canton. In 1989 he visited Kenya, Congo,
Cameroon, Ivory Coast and Nigeria, meeting and speaking
to as many people as he could to pass on the happiness of
loving and serving God in the Church. Another great joy
for him was to visit Poland, where he had already been
in 1979, to participate in the World Youth Day held in
Częstochowa from 12th to 16th August 1991. During
many of these pastoral journeys, he visited local shrines

of Our Lady to place Opus Dei and its members, as well as everyone in the different countries he went to, under her protection once again.

Alvaro del Portillo in Britain

In 1980 Mgr del Portillo came to Britain for several weeks in the summer. He had been before with St Josemaria for visits in five successive years, from 1958 to 1962. Now, as head of Opus Dei, his one concern was to talk to people about St Josemaria and encourage them to turn to his intercession and learn from his example. As yet, there were not many Opus Dei centres and they were all in England; Mgr del Portillo suggested that centres should be opened in Glasgow as soon as possible, to continue spreading the teachings of the Church and the message of love for God in and through ordinary everyday work. While he was in London, he made a pilgrimage to the shrine of Our Lady of Willesden, and another to Aylesford priory. He returned to the UK in 1985 and again in 1987, for briefer visits, and was able to see new developments taking shape. He encouraged the people of Opus Dei, and many others who came to see him, to be daring in undertaking new initiatives in the service of the Church.

Love for the Pope

Following St Josemaria's teaching, Mgr del Portillo loved, prayed for and supported each Pope, always seeing the

With Blessed John Paul II on 17th May 1992, the day of the beatification of the founder of Opus Dei.

Holy Father as the successor of Peter and the visible head of Christ's Church on earth. On 13th May 1981 the world was shocked by the attempted assassination of Pope John Paul II in St Peter's Square. From the moment he heard the news, Mgr del Portillo prayed intensely for him, and asked everyone to pray and offer reparation. He made time every day for the next few weeks to go to St Peter's Square to pray the Rosary for the Holy Father's recovery.

A personal prelature

The long search for the right canonical form for Opus Dei was finally crowned with success in 1982, when it became the first personal prelature in the Catholic Church. This type of organisation was originally defined by the Second Vatican Council. A prelature is an institution within the Church set up for a specific pastoral and apostolic purpose. It is "personal" because, unlike a diocese, it is not defined by territory, but by personal commitment. Before constituting Opus Dei as a personal prelature, Pope John Paul II consulted bishops worldwide and commissioned careful studies of all the aspects raised by their replies.

It was the culmination of many years' hard work and intense prayer by Mgr del Portillo, who had taken up the task on the death of St Josemaria. He already knew of the provisions made by the Second Vatican Council and the Code of Canon Law for the creation of personal prelatures, and he knew that this was, providentially, exactly the right structure for Opus Dei. He asked everyone in Opus Dei, and everyone who cared for it, to pray continually for this intention. In particular, he appealed to the Blessed Virgin Mary. He loved to make penitential pilgrimages to shrines of Our Lady, such as his first visit to Częstochowa, Poland, in 1979. He prayed the Rosary with intense devotion every day, and often gave people rosary beads, recommending the recipients to wear them out by constant use.

After the Holy Father had made Opus Dei into a personal prelature, Mgr del Portillo declared that he and everyone in Opus Dei could spend the rest of their lives giving thanks to God and to the Church for this outcome, which perfectly matched the characteristics of Opus Dei that St Josemaria had envisaged when he was first inspired to found it.

Ordained a Bishop

The Pope appointed Mgr del Portillo as the prelate of this new organisation, and, nine years later, on 6th January 1991, ordained him a bishop. Del Portillo, in his humility, did not see this new step as an honour for himself, but focused instead on the spiritual benefit it would bring to the whole of the Opus Dei prelature. He said:

"The prelate will receive the fullness of the Sacrament of Holy Orders: there will be a new outpouring of the Holy Spirit on the head of the Work, and, through the

Communion of Saints, on all of Opus Dei. It will mean a great impulse for the Work all over the world, a great gift from God, because the Prelate will be one of the College of Bishops and one of the successors of the Apostles."

Shortly after his consecration, he talked about how he had prayed during the solemn ceremony in St Peter's, during the Litany of the Saints.

"Lying there flat on the floor during the invocation of the saints, I meditated: 'We are poor worms, poor sinful men, and the outpouring of the Holy Spirit will come down on us, giving us the strength that we will need as the successors of the Apostles.' I prayed to God our Lord for faithfulness for everyone. I begged him: 'make us faithful, make us faithful!'"

With families in Ireland, 1980.

The Head of a Global Family

Family affection and concern for the sick

Opus Dei had received its characteristic spirit of fraternity and its sense of family from its founder. Del Portillo's biographer adds, "They were brought into being by the founder, but they are not dependent on his natural personality, warm as it was." Bishop Alvaro continued to take Opus Dei along the same path, with his own very different personality. He had a phenomenal memory and he knew the different people who made up the family of Opus Dei very well. No matter what great problems he had to deal with, he still showed his interest in and concern for all kinds of details, big and small, in the lives of his sons and daughters. He felt for their personal tragedies and really cared for the sick, following every stage of their illness, praying for them and helping them in every way that he could. In 1990 he was travelling from Barcelona to Pamplona in Spain, and stopped off at Saragossa to visit a daughter of his in Opus Dei who had been very badly burnt in an accident some months earlier. She was in an isolation ward in the burns unit and visitors were not allowed to her bedside, but Mgr del Portillo spoke to her by telephone, told her how much he was praying for her, and encouraged her to help people come closer to God by the power of her suffering. "Pain," she heard him saying, "is actually a caress from God," and those words, and his encouragement and affection, helped her faith enormously at that difficult time.

Works of mercy

Del Portillo's loving heart and deep concern for souls meant that he constantly encouraged Opus Dei members, together with other people, to set up works of mercy for those in need. "All of us", he wrote to his sons and daughters in Opus Dei in 1981, "have to make contact with those who are suffering, sick, destitute, alone or forsaken by all."

During his stay in DR Congo, in 1989, he encouraged his sons and daughters in Opus Dei and others to set up a hospital that offered high-quality care and was open to everyone. He saw this as one way among many to love and serve the Congolese people. The result was Monkole Hospital in the Mont-Ngafula district of Kinshasa, which opened in 1991 on a small scale and since then has grown little by little. One of its main areas of work is pregnancy and neo-natal care, in a part of the world where maternal and infant mortality have always been at unacceptably high levels. Monkole also offers AIDS treatment; works on HIV prevention; provides treatment for and research into sickle-cell anaemia; and provides training and facilities for basic hygiene, preventative medicine and primary health care in the most undeveloped parts of Kinshasa and the surrounding areas.

A similar initiative, also inspired by Mgr del Portillo, was the setting up in 1990 of the Niger Foundation Hospital in Enugu, Nigeria, which now offers medical care to those most in need. This hospital opened a rural outreach clinic at Aguobo-Iwollo in 2003, mainly supported by donations and fund-raising.

Neither did Del Portillo ignore the needs of those on his doorstep. In 1988 he suggested to some people in Opus Dei who were doctors and lecturers in medical sciences that there was a need for a university-level institution in Rome that would offer solutions to the reality of suffering and disease, in keeping with the Christian spirit of service to one's neighbour. As a result, the Campus Bio-Medico University Hospital was founded in 1991 and opened its doors in 1993, offering both state and private patients top-quality medical services that focus on the integral care of the individual - each patient, for example, is assigned a specific doctor and nurse for the whole of their stay in hospital - and on hygiene and cleanliness. It has since opened a special centre for the elderly. It is a teaching hospital, and the medical practice is informed by the latest medical research.

Social and educational initiatives

When Mgr del Portillo visited Mexico in 1983, he reminded the people of Opus Dei very forcefully about the social obligations of Catholics in countries where there is a wide gap between rich and poor. He knew very well all the work that they had already done in this field, but wanted to spur them on to aim for much more. As an immediate result, two more educational centres were opened in Mexico to provide education and training opportunities for people with limited resources.

Del Portillo was particularly concerned to bridge the gaps between rich and poor through education. Some of the initiatives that he inspired people of Opus Dei and others to set up for this purpose have been outstandingly successful in helping to solve the social problems of the environment in which they operate. Many of these institutions are in deprived districts or countries suffering high levels of disadvantage, especially in Africa, Latin America and the Philippines. In 1987, when Del Portillo visited the Philippines, there was much political unrest and violence. He encouraged people there to pray for peace and understanding. However, he pointed out that in that country, like many others, there were great social differences, poverty, and lack of educational opportunities for the poorest people. He advised those he met to do more themselves and to get others to do more, saying, "New social projects need to start as soon as possible." One of the results was a training centre for disadvantaged youths, the Center for Industrial Technology and Enterprise, in Cebu.

As well as feeling the urgency of helping the under-privileged, Del Portillo shared Pope John Paul II's concern for the need to raise the level of culture, education and intellectual thought in the world. He encouraged the establishment of universities and other teaching institutes geared to each country's particular needs. Examples of these were the University of La Sabana in Colombia, the Austral University in Argentina, the University of the Andes in Chile, and the University of Asia and the Pacific in the Philippines. All of this was done with a view to providing tertiary education with high standards of intellectual attainment, honesty, integrity and social responsibility, for the benefit of the whole country.

Friends

Alvaro del Portillo's natural friendliness gave rise to long-standing friendships with deep mutual affection. Among his lifelong friends were the maintenance man Emilio in Rome and the gardener Manolo in Spain. He was also on terms of firm, personal friendship with Pope Paul VI, Pope John Paul II, and very many other cardinals, bishops and priests. He was friends with so many people because he was a good friend; he kept in touch with them, when most people in his place would have decided they had too much work to do. He offered understanding, support and practical help in any way he could.

Helping priests

Del Portillo's concern for priests and the priesthood was shown once again in the Pontifical University of the Holy Cross, which started life as the Roman Academic Center of the Holy Cross in 1984 and became a Pontifical University in 1990. In the university and in the Sedes Sapientiae International Ecclesiastical College, also in Rome, thousands of seminarians and priests receive thorough doctrinal and spiritual formation. Del Portillo prayed constantly for all the priests in the Church, and when he made pastoral visits to different countries, he loved to meet the priests of the Priestly Society of the Holy Cross, and as many others as possible, to show them his affection and respect, and help them with his own zeal and counsel.

Love for Church institutions

Alvaro del Portillo was unfailingly generous with his time, experience and practical help when asked for advice. He helped various religious congregations at various times to obtain pontifical approval, to defend their own foundational charism, or to prepare documentation on the holiness of one of their members who had died. In return, several contemplative communities of women helped Opus Dei through their prayers. Del Portillo supported the causes for beatification for several religious, especially some of the Discalced Carmelites, and was one of those who wrote to Pope John Paul II requesting that the process of canonisation of Edith Stein be opened. She was beatified, to his great joy, in 1987 (and canonised as St Teresa Benedicta of the Cross in 1998).

In 1984, the founder of the movement Communion and Liberation, Mgr Luigi Giussani, wrote to Del Portillo, "The exquisite, operative charity you always have for us, as well as setting us an edifying example, makes us confident of receiving your advice and solidarity, as that of a father." Del Portillo loved to see the holiness of the Church flowering in all sorts of different ways; as he said once, "The fact that new lights are being lit makes us overflow with joy: it means that so many more people will be able to come to God."

Pastoral letters

Mgr del Portillo had taken up St Josemaria's habit of writing pastoral letters to all the people in Opus Dei to mark special events or share with them particular concerns that he felt. From 1984 onwards, amidst all the other work he had to do, he began writing them relatively short letters once a month, as a way of keeping in touch with the whole family of the Work, now that it was growing so large and spreading all over the world. His letters came straight from the heart. Each one provided a stimulus to a deeper relationship with God and more effective apostolate, offering pointers for a sincere examination of conscience. In them, he never failed to ask his spiritual sons and daughters for their prayers that he himself might be good and faithful.

A bishop who knew Del Portillo well said of him, "I always saw in him a Bishop similar to the great saints who ruled the Lord's flock, totally dedicated, despite his age, to his mission as Shepherd, and quick to follow the guidance of the Holy Father: a real example for Bishops the world over."

Devotion, a Great Joy, and His Last Day

Devotion to Our Lady

Alvaro had had a special love for Our Lady since he was a boy, and treated her as his heavenly Mother and a "short cut" to God. He always prayed to her, particularly for the holiness and faithfulness of everyone in Opus Dei. He habitually entrusted all his work to Our Lady so that she would present it to the Blessed Trinity, adding to it, as he said, the perfume of her loving, motherly hands so that it would be pleasing to God. His constant, trustful recourse to the Mother of God increased his closeness to each of the three Persons of the Blessed Trinity. He encouraged the people in Opus Dei to follow Our Lady's example, especially in humility and the theological virtues of faith, hope and love; and this was what he tried to do himself. On the various feast days of Our Lady he was as happy as though they were his own mother's birthday.

In thanksgiving for the fiftieth anniversary of the foundation of Opus Dei, Mgr del Portillo decided that 1978 would be celebrated as a Marian year by everyone in the Work. He extended this Marian year to 1979 and then again to 1980. During these three years he made a point of visiting shrines of Our Lady all over Europe, to pray for her help and protection. He did the same in 1987, a Marian Year for the whole Church. On these visits he always encouraged people to pray the Rosary together as a family.

In thanksgiving for Opus Dei being made a personal prelature, he made a special pilgrimage to Guadalupe, Mexico, in 1983. He stressed that "the best way to repay this gift from our Heavenly Mother is by being faithful to her Son Jesus." Mgr del Portillo, who had inherited a particular devotion to Our Lady of Guadalupe from his Mexican mother, said on that occasion that no reproduction or photograph of the original image that he had ever seen, really conveys the motherly expression of her face and in her eyes.

"The face of Our Lady of Guadalupe, which has very little paint, is extremely simple and has an expression of sweetness, humility, chastity, cleanness; and her eyes are compassionate, loving and somehow suffering at the same time. I think she must be suffering to see that people didn't believe Juan Diego, and she's looking at him with pity and loving tenderness. I thought about your sins and mine, and how affectionately Our Lady looks at us, because she's our mother, but at the same time, she's suffering … Let's not make our heavenly mother suffer."

Immersed in God

In order to help make Mgr Josemaria Escriva better known, Bishop Alvaro was interviewed at length by Cesare Cavalleri in 1992, and the interview was published in book form; the English translation, *Immersed in God*, appeared in 1996. In it, he talked in depth about the founder's love for God and the Church lived out to the point of heroism in his daily life, and the way he tackled difficulties of every sort. Bishop Alvaro's aim was to show that everyone could aspire to the heights of holiness just as St Josemaria had.

Beatification of St Josemaria

To Bishop Alvaro's great joy, the process of beatification of Mgr Josemaria Escriva came to a successful conclusion on 17th May 1992, when he was beatified by Pope John Paul II in St Peter's Square, in the same ceremony as that for Sister Josephine Bakhita (also later canonised). For Bishop Alvaro, the importance of this lay in the official recognition by the Church of the holiness that St Josemaria had achieved by his total response to God's grace at every moment of his life - in short, by loving God with deeds both big and small. By beatifying Josemaria Escriva, the Church was offering him as an example of holiness that could be imitated by the rest of the faithful.

Pilgrimage to the Holy Land and death

On 11th March 1994 Bishop Alvaro was eighty, and he was looking forward to celebrating in June the fiftieth anniversary of his ordination to the priesthood. On 14th March he fulfilled a longstanding ambition by setting off on a visit to the Holy Land, to spend a week of intense prayer retracing the footsteps of Jesus Christ during his life on earth. He and his companions visited the places of one Gospel scene after another, reading the relevant Gospel passages aloud on the way to prepare themselves to pray when they got there. With enormous devotion, Bishop Alvaro went to Nazareth, Ain Karim, Bethlehem, Lake Tiberias, the Mount of the Beatitudes, Cana, Mount Tabor, Bethany and Jerusalem. On 22nd March, he celebrated Holy Mass in the church next to the Cenacle. It was an immense privilege to celebrate Mass so close to the place of the Last Supper, and by an extraordinary act of God's providence, this was his last Mass on earth; he offered it, as was his custom, for the Holy Father and his intentions.

That afternoon he took the flight back to Rome, arriving home in the evening. In the early hours of the following morning he rang for help, saying that his heart was racing, and in spite of receiving prompt medical assistance, it became clear that he was dying. His closest assistant, Father Javier Echevarria, administered the Anointing of the Sick while Bishop Alvaro was still fully conscious. He was, as always, perfectly serene and cheerful, grateful for all that was being done for him - and calmly preparing for death. At four in the morning he died.

Two and a half hours later, Father Echevarria telephoned the Vatican and informed the Pope's secretary. Pope John Paul II offered his Mass that day for the repose of his friend's soul. In the afternoon, when Bishop Alvaro's body was resting in the prelatic church of Our Lady of Peace in Villa Tevere, the Holy Father came to pray before the body as a last gesture of affection. Bishop Alvaro was buried in the crypt of the church.

In June 2012 Pope Benedict XVI authorised publication of a decree stating that Alvaro del Portillo had practised the Christian virtues to an heroic degree, which meant that he was now Venerable Alvaro del Portillo, and in July 2013 Pope Francis signed a declaration that a miracle had been worked through Bishop del Portillo's intercession, putting him on track to be declared Blessed by the Catholic Church.

Bibliography

Bernal, S., *Alvaro del Portillo* (New York, Scepter, 1999)

Capucci, F., (ed.), *Perfil cronológico-espiritual del Siervo de Dios Mons. Alvaro del Portillo, Obispo y Prelado del Opus Dei (1914-1994)* (Rome, 2002)

de Azevedo, H., *Misión cumplida: Mons. Alvaro del Portillo* (Madrid, Palabra, 2012)

del Portillo, A., *On Priesthood: Consecration and Mission of the Priest* (Chicago, Scepter, 1974)

del Portillo, A., *Faithful and Laity in the Church: the bases of their legal status* (Shannon, Ecclesia Press, 1972)

Medina Bayo, J., *Un hombre fiel* (Madrid, Rialp, 2012)

Vazquez de Prada, A., *The Founder of Opus Dei*, volumes II and III (New York, Scepter, 2003, 2005)